CANOPY

ALSO BY

LINDA GREGERSON

CRITICISM

The Reformation of the Subject (1995)

Negative Capability (2001)

Empires of God, co-edited with Susan Juster (2011)

Linda

CAN

Gregerson

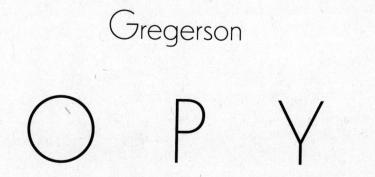

O P Y

An Imprint of HarperCollins*Publishers*

HarperCollins books may be purchased for educational, business,
or sales promotional use. For information, please email the Special
Markets Department at SPsales@harpercollins.com.

Ecco® and HarperCollins® are trademarks of HarperCollins Publishers.

FIRST EDITION

Designed by Emily Snyder

Library of Congress Cataloging-in-Publication Data has been applied for.
ISBN 978-0-358-67105-3 (Hardcover)
ISBN 978-0-358-62225-3 (Paperback)

22 23 24 25 26 LSC 10 9 8 7 6 5 4 3 2 1

For David Baker

And always, for Steven, Emma, Megan

Dulce lignum
Sweet the wood

Contents

CANOPY

Deciduous

Speak plainly, said November to the maples, say
        what you mean now, now

that summer's lush declensions lie like the lies
        they were at your feet. Haven't

we praised you? Haven't we summer after summer
        put our faith in augmentation.

But look at these leavings of not-enough-light:
        it's time for sterner counsel now.

It's time, we know you're good at this, we've
        seen the way your branched

articulations keep faith with the whole, it's time
        to call us back to order before

we altogether lose our way.   Speak
        brightly, said the cold months, speak

with a mouth of snow. The scaffolding is
        clear now, we thank you, the moon

can measure its course by you. Instruct us,
        while the divisions of light

are starkest, before the murmurs of con-
        solation resume, instruct us in

the harder course of mindfulness.
      Speak   truly, said April. Not just

what you think we're hoping to hear, speak
      so we believe you.

The child who learned perspective from the
      stand of you, near and nearer,

knowing you were permanent, is counting
      the years to extinction now. Teach her

to teach us the disciplines of do-less-harm. We're
      capable of learning. We've glimpsed

the bright intelligence that courses through the body
      that contains us.   *De +*

cidere, say the maples, has another face.
      It also means decide.

Love Poem

Once, my very best darling, the sea
        and the land were all one mass

and the light was confused and hadn't found
        a place to rest. And Emma, love,

my sister's eyes were not yet there to hold it all
        together since she hadn't yet been born and I

imagine though I never thought to ask them
        I believe they must have been afraid,

my own poor bid at being born so nearly having
        killed her, not my sister no our mother though

I see looking into your own two eyes that one
        as a matter of course entails the other. And

I don't even think I can properly call it love
        what I demanded what I had in mind I

wanted something mine and what you wish for if
        the gods see fit to grant it marks the limits

of your soul. And though the years have scoured
        the worst of what made me unfit for the gift,

had even then, when you were new, improved
        the odds, if all I could think with you

in my arms was taste of bile the thousand ways
         of harming you lest the world

should do it for me what's to become of me now
         she's gone. My sister, love, my one

and longed for only. You said
         because it has fallen on you to be my

comfort that's your daily job you said there's been
         science, the people in labs have done

brain scans and the thing we take for this-
         I-am-about-to-do is really just the flash

of the neurons in fear which has evolved to keep us
         safe. I didn't keep her safe. I left

her to the daily harms I might have seen them
         coming some of them one of the worst

in any case and then but that was different then
         the illness that had only left me bitten

took her altogether in its jaws. I thought sometimes
         that she had turned away from me,

I am frightened for you till you do.

Saint Sorry

Because she had no money and because
they called it a charity shop,
                    the woman whose ten-

week-old baby had finally died though of what
and why it couldn't be fixed she'd never
                    be able to understand,

she asked them there, the people at the charity shop,
would they give her a dress to wear for the service she
                    only had jeans,

and because they told her no,

                    my mother for years

would quietly bring our secondhand clothes
the twenty-odd miles to Portage where
                    if people were not kinder

in the aggregate, they hadn't yet flouted
the basic laws of human. Saint Vinny's
                    down the road she never

talked about why add to the shame which
means her trips to Portage were to our minds just
                    another of my mother's

minor oddnesses. I don't recall
who finally told me the story or how long
        she had been dead by then.

2.

Saint After-the-Fact. Saint Sorry-
I-Must-Have-Slept-through-the-Part-That-Mattered.
        And the time

I wouldn't eat it, food she'd cooked because
I'd asked for it. And every callow
        rudeness to a check-out clerk

I made her watch, like smearing mud
on linen. If these are the screens imagine the things
        I did that I won't talk about.

That grocery cart abandoned in the parking lot?
When you see me pushing it back to the store
        think penance in a faithless age.

3.

"It's not so much the terror when the world as they
know it is broken in two (six-year-olds,
        two-year-olds,

snatched at the border and carted off to god-
knows-where) it's what dawns on them later:
        this isn't

some terrible rupture in the-way-the-world-is-meant-
to-work it's the way it has always
                              been (you can see it in

their faces) and will always be. Their eyes go flat.
So that's when I had my money shot I
                        filed the JPEG went back

to our dreary motel (plaid carpets!) and ordered a double
scotch. Camera in the bottom of my shoulder bag
                        glad for the dark."

4.

In the novel I love, years later, when
the killing has not stopped but only shifted to other
                        fronts the girl

who of course is no longer a girl and knows
as once she had only surmised
                        how much

of the wreckage is beyond repair
the girl who is older now and for a moment
                        distracted turns

and with her shoulder dislodges a glass that
falls as glasses do to the floor but just
                        before the floor

on the other side of the globe the boy
who of course is no longer a boy and yet
                        endowed

with the grace it takes a boy to catch
a fallen object, say
     a shiny piece of

cutlery, while it's still in the air
extends his arm
    and does.

5.

Of Paradise, wrote Mandeville, I cannot
properly speak, for in all my travels
     I was not there.

Variations on a Phrase by Cormac McCarthy

Like the carpenter whose tools were so dull
he couldn't for the life of him devise a miter joint

Like the mattress left out on the curb all night

Like the woman
so fallen out of practice she can no longer sing from the hymnal
Like the smoker on the scaffolding

Like the sleeper on his cardboard on the pavement Like the rain

Like the dog whose human so loves her   Whose hip
will never heal again
Like the dog who trembles in pain on her leash whose human
so loves her he cannot bear to let her go

Like the takeout tossed into the bin for recycling   Like
the crosswalk the postbox   the flashing light

Like the beggar whose accordion knows only
the single musical phrase   Like the air
with its particulates   Like the idling bus

Like the cherries at the fruit stall   Like the cyclist   Like
the bus   Like the cyclist Like his cell phone Like the bus

Like the beggar so bored with the music he
has never sounded out the rest of the song   *Like the carpenter*

whose work went so slowly for the dullness of his tools
he had no time to sharpen them

Melting Equestrian

(CAVENDISH SQUARE)

There's the irony intended and the irony added like
           icing on top: fill the air with

           sweetness, scented-soap-on-a-
plinth, while the rains come down, and be gone

within a twelvemonth. As
           the sculptor proposed. But the rains

           were slow to come that year
and the public less fickle than planned and so

this butcher-on-horseback, copy of a copy, stood
           for forty-eight months

           in eloquent tribute, limb
by limb, to the powers of necrosis. When I saw

him first I was baffled by the strutwork,
           the sticking-out, simplified

           bones of steel that should
have been covered by flesh. Prosthetics-made-

political? I was only half mistaken.
           The prince (he was of course

           a prince) had been the hero
of Culloden, thus Sweet William to his fellow

defenders-of-England. Hence
        the statue. Hence,

                as will happen from time to time
        when we finally look at aftermath, the hundred

        years of empty plinth. The hundred and more. I
                simplified. So much

                for the link between memory
        and shame. But this talking-to-the-past knowing

        better, which (we've read the statistics we've
                some of us walked the battlefields)

                we have to imagine we do, at least
        the knowing part, is quite another thing than knowing

        better in time. First roundshot, then grapeshot, then
                hand-to-hand on marshy

                ground where, as they had been
        trained to do, the English in formation thrust their

        bayonets not forward but into the enemy on the
                right. And then

                the butchery in the highlands.
        I have a hunch, despite

        what they tell me on Wiki, that the tactic at Culloden
                wasn't new at all. Some

Scythian surely or Roman-in-
Gaul had thought of that angle before? Whereas

I tend to trust the news release: the scented
        soap provided etc by

Scented Soaps etc which you
can purchase at your local shop. The arts and the

ever-in-need-of-augmentation art of patching up
        public subsidy.

The lead-and-gilt original
was paid for by a single admiring donor while

the donor's troops (he too was a leader of men)
        were shipped to Ireland in rags.

Provisions, it seems, had gone
astray. As will attention. For every harm

I manage to hold in mind I let a hundred slip.

Bearded Iris

I.

A sort of synaesthetic pun: the purples
          smell like grapes when grapes

still had a smell, and remnants
          of fertility, which we

in an excess of ever-more-ease
          have banished from our tables.

A throwback then, like Concords on the trellis
          below the swing. The sibling

blossoms—firstborn, second,
          opening in succession—ought

to be a sign of comfort-in-community but
          look how the youngest

carry the browning corpses on their shoulders. As
          so often is the case with us.

I used to think Siberians played the better part
          all round: the solitary

flourish then the choir of stately verticals
          till fall. What was it

I thought the world could provide?
          Mortality without the mess?

2.

My father was the oldest and therefore
          expected to have

a leather heart. They were farmers
          animals died.

But when Eddie's favorite dog got old it was
          Olaf's job

to go into the woods with a gun.
          So neither late

nor early are we spared. Good dog,
          it followed where it was led.

3.

Ruffled falls and ruffled shoulders —
          a garden

of children in pinafores. *Nor nocent yet,*
          John Milton wrote,

the better to remind us we can imagine
          no such thing.

He couldn't have been much more than one,
          my father, in the photograph,

not speaking yet, first haircut still
          some months away. How

in the world did she manage?
>White bloomers, white smock,

they would have been washed when the chores
>were done, the iron —

I've held it — heated on the cookstove.
>Photographer once

a year. The sheer hard work
>to posit a state of cleanliness.

4.

Stigma, stamen, ovary, beard: flaunted
>devotion to making-

more-of-the-same. If the dog does not
>whimper

but lies down and covers its head
>with its paws

and the man with the gun isn't much for
>words, where

do you go for plotline? If
>the man

who built the trellis and the swingset too
>and taught a child to count

while he pushed wasn't frightened
>of death for his own sake but

would say we had it coming, all of us,
        better a bit

too soon than all this sordid hanging on,
        will the child

be better equipped for — what-do-we-call-them? —
        years-to-come?

First adding, then subtraction, then before
        you know it,

remainders. The parts that can't be made to fit.

The Wayfarer

(HIERONYMUS BOSCH, 1516)

When the wings of the triptych are open as
    must often
        be the case he's split in two. As in

another sense he was at his inception since
    the painter
        having liked his own creation or

engaged by a client determined to claim
    the credit for
        another of the same produced this

duplicate some fifteen years after the first.
    He's older here,
        the man with the woven pack on his

back, he's still warding off the malevolent dog.
    And measuring
        progress left to right as one might read

the middle distance with its cautionary
    portraits
        of pleasure and vice. Note the gallows

with its ladder, note (much closer) the
    scattered remains
        of a horse. The part I can't quite

solve for is the little bridge. A piece
        of civic
                courtesy, so notably missing in most

of the view. There's even a handrail albeit one
        so flimsy
                that a traveler would be ill-advised to

use it. Still. The thought that counts.
        The bridge itself
                not timber as the makeshift

construction would in the usual course of
        things entail
                but quarried stone which wants

a story to explain it. Repurposed perhaps
        from a grave-
                yard or a fallen church?

Waste not want not, common
        in the countryside.
                And sweeter too for messing up

the parable: journey of the soul etcetera
        pitfalls avoided
                dangers survived. And sometimes

just for fellowship the human gift
        of making do.
                That the panel itself was once

a living tree is what the living rely on
       to give us a date.
              Vicissitudes of sun and rain

encoded in growth rings for all to see.
       Your time here,
              traveler, scarcely leaves a mark.

Sleeping Bear

(SLEEPING BEAR DUNES NATIONAL LAKESHORE,
LEELANAU COUNTY, MICHIGAN)

I.

The backstory's always of hardship, isn't it?
                No-other-choices and hoping-for-better
on foreign shores. A minute ago, as measured

by the sand dunes here, the shipping lanes were thick
                with them, from Hamburg, Limerick, towns
along the Oslofjord, and lucky to have found

the work. The Michigan woodlands hadn't been denuded yet
                (a minute ago) so one of the routes was
lumber and the other tapped a prairie's worth

of corn. There's a sort of cushioned ignorance that comes
                of being born-and-then-allowed-to-live-in-
safety so I used to think it must have been more

forgiving here, less brutal than the brutal North Atlantic
                with its fathoms and its ice. But no.
The winds, the reefs, the something-to-do-with-

narrower-troughs-between-the-waves and lakes like this
                are deadlier than oceans: in
a single year the weather claimed one in every

four. We come for the scale of it: waters without
                a limit the eye can apprehend and — could
there be some mistake? — aren't salt. Dunes

that dwarf pretension which if falsely consoling is right and
            good. Where commerce lifts its sleeping head.
      If I had the lungs for diving I expect I'd be there

too among the broken ribs and keels. Visitors need
            a place to sleep and something to fill up the
      evenings, it's natural, the people in town

need jobs. Calamity-turned-profit in tranquility. My
            father's father's father was among the ones
      who did not drown. Who sold his ship

and bought a farm.

2.

What is it about the likes of us? Who cannot take it in
            until the body of a single Syrian three-
      year-old lies face down on the water's edge? Or this

week's child who, pulled from the rubble, wipes
            with the back and then the heel of his small
      left hand (this time we have a video too) the blood

congealing near his eye then wipes (this is a problem,
            you can see him thinking Where?) the hand
      on the chair where the medic has put him.

So many children, so little space in our rubble-strewn
            hearts. In alternative newsfeeds I am
      cautioned (there is history, there is such a thing

as bias) that to see is not to understand. Which (yes, I know,
            the poster child, the ad space, my consent-
      to-be-governed by traffic in arms) is true and quite

beside the point. The boy on the beach, foreshortened
                    in the photograph, looks smaller than
            his nearly three years would make him, which

contributes to the poignancy. The waves have combed his
                    dark hair smooth. The water on the shingle, in-
            different to aftermath, shines.

3.

There was once, says the legend, a wind-borne fire or as
                    some will recount it a famine and
            a mother bear with her two cubs was driven

into the lake. They swam for many hours until the
                    smaller of the cubs began to weaken and,
            despite all the mother could do, was drowned,

then the second cub also, so when the mother reached
                    the shore which then as now betokened
            a land of plenty she lay down with her face

to the shimmering span whose other side was quite
                    beyond her powers of return. The islands
            we call Manitou, the one and then the other, are

her cubs, she can see them, we go to them now by ferry.
                    We are not
            the people to whom the legend belongs.

4.

And even on my city block. There has always been suffering,
                    both little and large. *But does it
            compare to mine?* Yours is nothing.

I saw the woman running. I heard her scream.
              You did nothing.
     She said please she said help me we all stood still.

You all stood still. *It took us a minute to figure it out,*
              by then they were down
     the street. And then? *The men were on bikes,*

I didn't think that happened here. That wasn't
              my question. *Whatever*
     they'd taken had made her quite desperate, I've

never heard a scream like that. Then you? *Then we*
              went on with our evening.

                    5.

Stroke of the pen. 16:42 on a Friday. Say you were
              already in the air.
     You've given away your blankets, your

tent, you thought you'd seen the last of camps. Or say
              it was your buddy from
     the 82nd Airborne: interpreter, ally,

engineer. Targeted twice because of what he did
              for you. His papers are no good now,
     your promises were lies. *Detrimental,* says

the president. *Malicious intent.* Says, *Only those*
              who love us. That's
     your favorite part.

6.

If a spirit — call him Manitou — takes pity on a
          family of bears or, more
     to the point, if humans imagine they share

the earth with bears who are worthy of pity and
          a cognizant spirit however
     remote with pity to spare, why then

why then a sand dune may be more than sifted
          silica. The wind goes on with its
     sorting, the lake bed cradles its dead.

But part of the language the glacier used
          to speak to the sculpted substrate will
     include this bit of sediment.

We didn't mean to fail you. We were here.

The Long Run

A woman's face—I know how this sounds—but women's
faces generally they have a different way
of breaking down. I don't say good or bad. Whereas

a man, some men, when you see that tightening
at the corners of his mouth that's how you know.
A little tightening, everything at stake. And one

of them was like that, talking about that terrible November
day. How many ways can you ruin a life?
Take an eighteen-year-old boy, for example, send him

halfway around the world to kill civilians but
encourage him first to play with the little ones, soccer
field maybe, meet with the elders, what-do-you-need—

the whole road-tested hearts-and-minds. A few of them
get killed then, not the locals but his buddies, and
their new lieutenant issues a "change of rules."

And now they're murderers, the boy and all the other
boys who thought they'd been lucky to stay alive. For a
while it seems there's something still to hang on to:

a trial, a chance to testify, the murderer-in-chief in jail.
How many ways can you ruin a life?
"A hero," says the president. And, as the law if not

the cause the law once had in mind allows, turns inside
out what all of them knew and, knowing, did. November.
Calls it Pardon. The ones who were guilty of nothing

still dead. That place on the other side of the world
more broken than it was. And the face I'm trying to talk
about, maybe you've seen one like it too.

2.

There's always a moment before the moment when nothing
is ever the same again. The moment before the leg

of my uncle's overalls got caught in the baler pick-up. The
moment before the moment you decided to tell your lover

the truth. The moment before the horses panicked, the
moment before the acid splashed, the moment before

the driver got distracted by his GPS. How was a fourteen-
year-old girl supposed to know what it meant? It wasn't her

job to answer the phone, her job was the attendance sheets.
The phone rings, she's a dutiful child, *Three minutes*

says the man on the line, hangs up. "But it wasn't," she
tells us, "three minutes at all." She's come to give us a tour

of the church: the basement where the four of them (Addie
Mae tying her dress sash) had just finished morning lessons,

the staircase to the office and the nave with its pews. You'd
never know unless you knew already that the stained glass

windows, all but one, had been replaced. "Fifteen steps,"
she says, from where she'd been to where she made it

when the bomb went off. "I can count them in my sleep.
Fifteen."

3.

Or slowly, the other irrevocables.
The teething infant, chips of paint. The water that flows

through the aging pipes. Is it something peculiar to us,
do you think, this science-will-fix-it, somebody-somewhere-

will-figure-out-the-cleanup way of burning through our one
shared life. At the turn of the century in which I was born

the topsoil here in Iowa was sixteen God-sent inches
deep. We're down to half. Three tons lost

per acre per year because we like our groceries cheap.
I've sometimes taken comfort in the long run, in

the long run some worthier species will, fate willing,
inherit the earth. In the long run the creek bed . . . the

coastline . . . the karst . . . In the long run the fern and the
nautilus speak a single fractal language. My father loved

the ginkgos on the statehouse lawn, the former statehouse,
Greek Revival, columns and cupola painted to look like stone.

And no more native here than we are, or the ginkgo, but he
loved the trees. The species coexisted with the dinosaurs.

A ginkgo in Hiroshima survived the atom bomb. It must
have been unforgivable, the thing I said that made him cut

their visit short. Forgetting hasn't fixed it.

Not So Much an End as an Entangling

(TOM UTTECH, OIL ON LINEN, 2016)

I.

And then the animals began to flee
                              from right
          to left across the surface of the visual

plane, the birds in great number, owl
                              and osprey,
          red-necked grebe,

the nuthatch, the nighthawk, the warbler in
                              eleven
          kinds. And that's when we began to

understand because it wasn't normal, wasn't
                              what you
          expect to find, the eaters and the likely-

to-be-eaten in a single frame. *Despised*
                              the ground,
          our poet says, *intelligent of seasons.* And

the sixth day too, when creatures of the earth
                              began to walk
          the earth, proposes a thought-scape of

nothing-needs-to-die-that-I-might-live.
                              But that was
          then and in the painting it is more

like now, desiccated needles on a desiccated
                              branch. If creation-
          with-pinions appears to fly below as well as

in the sky, that's simply a trick of vantage point,
                              the better
          to accommodate the interlocking logic

of the whole, as when
                              eternity
          is broken into pieces we construe as plot.

So timber wolf and white-tailed deer and indigo
                              bunting below
          which is to say between, perspective

having turned the three dimensions into two,
                              all of them
          fleeing, right to left, as from (since they, who

are *intelligent of seasons*, are the first to know) from
                              imminent
          disaster, which has made the lesser enmities
                              moot.

                              2.

When I was a child it was the numbers I couldn't
                              get out of
          my head, so many billions, so little time

to make it stop. A single patch of ground, say, just
                              from here
          to the wall: how many of us, if we took turns

lying down, could fit? I didn't think water or waste
                              or work,
            I just thought how many standing and how

many minutes the others would get to rest. Only later
                              did
            the obvious answer occur to me: I won't

be here, and then the panic would stop. *But have*

                            3.

I now seen death he wondered and the angel said,
                              you've scarcely
            seen its shadow, look: the winged-ones, furred-

ones fleeing from right to left, as from the
                              names that you
            in all your fond first powers bestowed.

There was water in the reedbeds (think of it,
                              water still), the sun
            still rose, the snail-foot exuded

its mucus. And then the angel pulled, just slightly,
                              on one of the threads
            composing the linen

the painter had tacked to his stretcher. What is it
                              you love
            that has not been ruined because of you.

Love Poem

I.

Once, my very best darling, the sea
       and the land were all one mass

and the light was confused and hadn't found
       a place to rest. And, Megan, love,

my sister's eyes were not yet there to hold it all
       together since she hadn't yet been born so when

the world dropped out from under us and no one,
       not the on-calls with their CAT scans, not

the sovereign souls who monitor
       the twilit room where newborns come to die

or live, when no one could tell us if you
       would be one of the lucky ones able to

walk and speak and only this, the one
       unstinted blessing fate had given us to

give you was a sister in whose eyes you were
       the sun and moon, it meant we all no matter

what befell us all
       had solid ground.   Pity the part

we think we do on purpose.

2.

When Karen was dying and books had shut
       their doors to her, she could still make out the

puzzle of knit and purl. I'm keeping it simple,
       she said, although the pattern

emerging beneath her fine hands did not
       look simple to me. An

A. A B. An alphabet. And all in the single
       color, milk. The letters distinguished

by only the altered stitchwork so
       the nursery would be beautiful.

Whichever of the children has a baby first,
       she said, she loved

the future, no matter she wouldn't be there.

3.

Second-born. As fateful as the transit
       to light and air or so you've often tried

to teach me I will never properly understand.
       But I know

how the hair at your temples curls in
       summer when the air is moist. As if

she'd been returned to me.
       I must have had some under-the-radar

notion even then when we were children how
       that little looseness threw

my petty masteries in the shade. And so
       the joy of it was lost on me. Till you.

I'm the only person living who
       remembers her childhood curls.

Horse in a Gas Mask

Browband   cheekpiece   throatlatch
          bit.
Plus all the links and leathers for holding

this extra part on. We're meant to be accustomed
          to the bodies
in the mud. We've seen the documentaries,

we've read about the mustard gas. We know
          they're only
actors on a union wage. What is it

about the horse that falls — is that the way
          to put it — falls
just slightly out of solution here? Precipitate,

noun. That fails to hold its peace within the fiction.
          There will
have been a handler on the set, there are rules.

The barbed wire won't have torn his flank.
          You can train
a horse to stagger. Maybe. Check

the delicate ankles later on. But this ghastly
          reproduction
of a ghastly piece of now-you're-allowed-to-

breathe-again, it isn't so wholly removed
          from the world
as in a better world would be the case. You've seen

the newsreels? Everything black-and-white back
          then, the one
man's hand on the first man's shoulder, next

man's hand on his, and then the whole retreating
          line of them, gassed,
bandages over their eyes. It seems

the horses could go blind as well, no help for it,
          something about
the goggles and their fogging up. So in

this latter-day story-by-means-of-moving-pictures
          one part
punctures the set-to-music consolations of

it's-all-a-reenactment-with-a-proper-arc.
          Cantle
Pommel   stirrup   girth.

All suited to our purposes.
          Camera.
Liquid eye.

Fragment

What,
said the general, with all his stars, can I do

for you, soldier. And the boy with no legs
and half an arm

said *Get me back*
to my squad, Sir.

What, said the Catholic to the Welshman,
are you doing in

Belfast.
And the Welshman in his British-Army-

issued gear: *I didn't have money for school.*
We imagined,

in the middle of that
other war, when we were young, that righteousness

would see us through. We chartered buses to
Washington, we sang

in the cathedral *Dies*
irae who will plead for me / when even the just

need mercy. We had no real idea what the singing
meant. My cousin

on the phone last week —
she volunteers at shelters, she's been out of a job

for months — called them riots and — this might
as easily be

me but for the path I swear
I won't confuse with essence — and

I heard her get his name wrong too, this latest,
nearest

murdered man.
Great trembling *quantus tremor* what is hidden

shall be revealed.   And we
with our what-can-I-do-to-

help and our thinking
the insight began with us: bound to act and bound

to be not enough.

Archival

If the curator should wish, for example,
        to save for later scrutiny (or

wonder, wonder's worthy too) a once-
        ubiquitous download for

disbursing the forces of Christendom
        or evading the enemy's land mines

or colonizing Mars and if, as is all
        but certain, the program depends

on software run by hardware no longer
        extant, if reconstructions work too

well, eliding the awkward temporal gap
        between keystroke and pixelated

body count, how will they know
        what it's like to be us? If even

the ditches along our abandoned railroad
        spurs have long succumbed to

never-any-water, how will they know
        what we mean by July?

(when the cornflowers first appear) (when
        gladly the parched eye quenches

its thirst in blue). For providence, in lieu
       of the kind we used to think

we trusted in, we've built a Global
       Seed Vault on an island in the

Arctic Sea. There are rules. The seeds
       aren't "owned" but "stored"

and only the donors of origin have access.
       (That will tell them something too.)

So maize and eggplant, lotus root and
       cabbage in potentia for the world

to come. Assuming survival of people who
       remember what the seeds are for

and something that passes for topsoil.
       Permafrost, five hundred meters at

present, and sleeping tectonics below. Site
       well above what's likely to be a

flood zone when the ice caps melt. It must
       have helped with costs a bit to build

the vault where once we mined for coal.
       They'll credit us with irony.

Interior, 1917

The dining hall for instance: open roof beams,
    open screens, and yard upon yard

of clean swept hardwood flooring, it
    might almost be a family camp.

And likewise in the sleeping room: expanse
    of window, paneled wall, and the

warmth implied by sunwash, only softened
    here by half-drawn shades. You know

the kind?—dark canvas on a roller, in my
    memory the canvas is always green. What I

couldn't have guessed, except for the caption:
    the logic behind the double row of well-

made beds. I'd like just once to have seen
    his face, the keeper of order who

thought of it first: a "prostitute" on either side
    of each of those women demanding

the vote. And "Negro," as though
    suffrage were white by default. *You thought*

your manners and your decent shoes would
    keep you safe? He couldn't have known

how much we'd take the lesson to heart.
    At the workhouse in Virginia they'd started

the feedings with rubber tubes. Not here.
    Or not that we've been told. The men

all dying in trenches in France. A
    single system, just as we've been

learning for these hundred years. Empty
    of people, the space looks almost benign.

Epithalamion

For Susan and George

The beautiful geometry the trees become
        each winter here
is beginning to blur at the edges a bit

        and the robin we think
must be a little deranged has for the third time
        in as many years

returned from wherever she goes for sun and
        resumed
her attacks on the window. She's at it every

        day, feet first,
as though to scatter an enemy host
        or seize

some last essential. And on the theory she's been
        deceived
by the visual field, we've tried removing the

        blinds, the screen,
and once in desperation taping a page of the New
        York Times

to the glass. No luck. She is relentless as
        the warming earth.
Sweet lake, abide our lingering here.

The four-
footed creature who year after year leaves
          a wreckage

of yolk-smeared shell beneath the weeping
          larch where year
after year our robin restores her nest

          must come
by night. *Sweet lake*. He too has his work
          in the world, or so

I've tried to think. The window refuses to
          moralize.
But wedding songs require a point of view

          and we,
when grief has had its way with us, are
          all the more

stubborn in matters of joy. The joy
          that has been
untouched by grief is precious and

          protectionless.
This chosen joy — *Sweet lake, abide* — is
          rarer still. And shared.

Ram of the Week

Long before I knew him, when the world was young,
my husband, all hundred and fifteen pounds of him, staged

a dazzler
            of a once-in-a-lifetime thirty-yard-line save.

The details are mainly lost on me, to this day I can barely
follow the ball, but something about *committed to the tackle* and

lateral pass became the skinniest guy on defense taking two

men out. And thus the title for one glorious
autumn afternoon and seven days to come.

It's spring now. Baseball has gone virtual. And Steven,

armed with mask and gloves, has commandeered our weekly
expeditions to the grocery store (my lungs a co-

morbidity). (I'm banished from even unpacking the bags.)
No shoulder pads, no helmet. Just

the ever-unflagging taking-care essential to him

as breathing. In
a world where every breath I take is luck.

Narrow Flame

Sun at the zenith. Greening
       earth.
   Slight buckling of the left

hind leg. And all this while
      the girl
   at his ear *good boy* and now

the hip giving way and mildly as
      was ever
   his wont the lovely

heft of him lists toward the field
      that minutes ·
   ago was still so sweet for

grazing and *good boy* and on the
      ground
   now where the frightening

last shudder of lungs that we've been
      warned about
   does thank you darling does

not come and feeling for a pulse
      no pulse
   and warning us touching

the liquid eye which does not
      close which
   means the slender needle with

its toxic everlastingness has done
       its job
   good boy unbuckling the

halter lifting the beautiful head
       to her
   lap and all this while the girl . . .

If the Cure for AIDS,

said someone in that earlier pandemic, were
a glass of clean water, we couldn't save half the people here.

                        If half
the workers at Tyson Meats come down with the virus we still
have a plan for protecting the owners from lawsuits.

                 If the phone in the farmhouse
rings when it's long past dark and the milk . . .
           If the tanks at the co-op are full . . .

If milk dumped into the culvert makes you think of death.

My neighbor drove to Lansing in his pickup, I expect
you've seen the photos too. The statehouse floor. The rifles. He

          had just culled half his herd. And while
we're casting about for ways to summon normal, I've been
watching footage of the day-old chicks.
                  The hundred and sixteen

thousand buried alive, it seems we can't afford the feed.
         Or can't afford the falling price of
chicken. I'm mostly confused

             by the articles meant to explain.
Look at the spill of them, dump truck into the pre-
dug ditch, the mewling yellow spill of them, still

          in the down we find adorable. Red earth.
Impassive skyscape. Skittering
        bits of agitation on the body of the whole.

A Knitted Femur

First evidence
        that one who ought to have died first,
of hunger,
        of thirst, in the jaws of something

hungrier,
        lived long enough to heal.
Not pottery
        not crafted tool but simply

this far-from-simple
        testament to taking care. The question
had been civilization:
        early remains. Excavate the layered earth

and lo, if you're
        asking the question with an open mind:
a carbon-dated 15,000-
        year-old sign. Which opens an obvious

thought-stream when
        a father-of-six or daughter-of-your-cousin
gets a job telling shoppers
        to put on a mask. What's the starting salary

for getting shot?
        I've been reading about resilience and
how viruses
        are good at this. Block them at one pass

they'll adapt
  and find a work-around. Kill the host
they'll find another.
   Anger must be like that too. When I tried

to sign up for the
  listserv I was shuttled to another screen
and asked to "confirm
   humanity." I checked the box.

Slip

Liquid alignment of fabric and outer
        thigh. *Slip.*
Which mimics the thing it's meant to allow.
        Passage

of air on either side of the tongue whose meat
        as if
to thicken the likeness of substance and sound
        meets just

that plot of upper palate behind the teeth.
        And yet
at normal speed the very aptness loses its full
        bouquet.

"Salomé was wearing red pumps and the palest of
        pale blue
satin slips." I would in my predictable girlhood
        have much

preferred a word I took to be scented like Giverny:
        "Salomé
was wearing red pumps and a pale blue satin
        chemise."

It's taken me all this time to hear the truer
        difference —*slip*—
which only wants a little lingering in the mouth
        to summon how it

thinks about the contours of the body. So the
        speed of it—
slip—and the lingering can resume their proper tug-
        of-war. The boy

they'd had the wit to cast as Salomé, both nude
        and may-as-well-be-
nude, was every inch presentable, flawless, as
        though one

might live in the body and feel no shame. No
        wonder,
forced to endure as they did the reek of the tidal
        Thames, our

predecessors took this for the universal object of
        desire.
The history of the English stage right there in the
        slippage between not-

quite and already over and gone. And yes I
        get
the part about predation the grooming in all of its
        sordid detail,

I was never half so fair as this but fair enough
        to have been
fair game. In a town with limited options.
        I've spent

more than half my life trying to rid myself
        of aftermath
so let me be enchanted now. Youth at a safe
        remove.

Uncorrected Vision

As in
the floating interim before

the last sweet wash of anesthesia . . .
as
in childhood when it's not your fault . . .

as when the one whose thoughts you might but
will not be obliged to hear

is simplified to silhouette
bright window behind him   unstable

margin
at the darkness you take to be his throat

suggesting
speech or
struggle you cannot tell which and

(here's the blessing) needn't

Lumberyard on one side, gas pumps
on the other, three

houses in between. And ours the one with the
thicket of broken-down mowers out back.

A train spur for the lumberyard

a highway instead of a street. The rattle
        of couplings and thud of the tires

when the long-hauls cross the sunken tracks.

        My mother's tulips

      trying to make it decent.
                      Note

how punctuation slips back in.
        To indicate control.

     And yet
this link of well-being to blinded-by-sunlight solitude-

       with-people-near.
       It would have been a birthday or the Fourth

of July, kitchen chairs on the lawn, the women
        bringing food out. The child

     molester who married my aunt. The child
   molester who lives next door. But I

     don't have to know that yet.
There's someone else in charge.

As on this 767 on the tarmac   while
          they check the engines one last time

      Two aisles and five coach seats away
              the sunstruck window
the talking   if that's what he's doing   man

      I used to think I wanted the world exclusively
        in focus
                 I
        am learning otherwise.

Scandinavian Grim

Vocal in the ordinary course of things
                on the vastly
                superior merits of having lapsed

from a less-for-all-its-flaws-deforming
                form
                of Christian worship my husband

has so far sweetly refrained from using
                this one
                as a case in point. But what

were we to do? When my mother said
                Linda
                and looked that look, I could

see it all before me. *Linda*, she said, *We
                can't
                insult him*. We'd made alternate plans.

But the pastor — call him Grimly — had for
                three days.
                shown up at her bedside to pray

while we muted "Take the A Train" (her
                favorite)
                and practiced the seven stages of

awkward. I'll spare you the history
                of the Ladies'
                Aid. But consider my cousin Paul,

good soul, who drives out every Sunday in
        the predawn
        dark to light the furnace they can't

afford to run all week. And in summer mows
        the graveyard.
        Consider the graveyard, its Emmas

and Gregers in modest rows, including
        the boy
        whose team of horses panicked when

the train came through. Now imagine what
        it took
        to loosen my mother's allegiance,

whose one fixed faith was kindness.
        Even her funeral,
        she'd rather defer. In the end,

though I ought to confess some not-quite-
        fully-in-the-spirit-of-
        my-mother back-and-forthing, Pastor

Grimly found he couldn't in conscience
        welcome
        the gathering we had in mind.

So rights-of-first-refusal for his dignity,
        and thankfully back
        to Alternate Plans, which included

something more like love. Can I count on my
        husband's forbearance
   forever? Probably not. But maybe

I'll lighten up for a while on the
        hostage-to-hypocrisy rant
   about pardon.

Environmental

I had the right of way — on foot —
and therefore by definition was able

to pause without braking, resume without
a burst of petrochemicals, besides

the day was mild and all before me which
did not in the end do a bit

of good by the time the puzzled motorist
had stopped, had gestured,

seen me gesture in return, believed me.
Great boots! he called as he rounded

the corner. Net loss
for the fight against global warming.

But let me revise the part about no
bit of good.

When Nothing but Tree

can be seen in the tree though the dogs
unmistakably indicate, when clearly

the canopy calls to them and days
have passed before you've even begun,

when nothing in the undergrowth has
prompted so much as a whimper, you

must turn your thoughts to the other bank.
Scent from a living body will be carried

on the wind. Scent from a corpse in the
river spreads like oil. But say

the return-to-elements has started just
beyond that rise. The body is cold,

the scent like a river seeks lowest ground
becoming part of the river itself which the

trees in turn imbibe and, drawing upward,
change to living green.

The one you seek is now an exhalation.
As the dogs, intelligent beyond our wildest

reckoning, have told us. Have
been telling us.

In Basel, on a panel made of limewood,
emphatically unrisen,

the body of Christ lies in its frame as in
a coffin. Thwarted verticals. And strung

along a fault line where the pigment-
in-egg-yolk old way meets the pigment-

in-linseed new, the flesh
breathes beauty as only

that-which-is-liable-to-perish can breathe.
The green-going-black of face, of feet,

of visible hand confirm: no going back to
what you were. How is it

the linen on which he lies so clearly
discloses a pallet of stone (and hence

the catalog title — *entombed*) which means
the coffin I've imagined (warmer

framewood) must be pity's crafted after-
thought. Or argument. The wholly

this-world begging to differ
with all we've been taught to hope for.

1521: the heretic from Wittenberg
refuses to recant though the question

has not yet turned to *presence* or *real*.
Sit down at my table (*my body my*

blood) and I on your behalf will paint
a picture. Note the gaping nostril, gaping

mouth, the other mouth of the wound in his
side, the cradle of the abdomen. You see

how disproportionate I've made his length,
the better to seal credulity. It's fifteen

hundred twenty-one. "It is known,"
writes my informant, "that the artist used

a body retrieved from the Rhine (citation
needed)." And either

the fish had not eaten the open eye or
Holbein in his studio restored it. Never

elsewhere, says the limewood, never
blind. Behold

the nearer case for mystery. I'm here to praise.

Notes

"SAINT SORRY"
Section 4: Michael Ondaatje, *The English Patient*, 1992.

"VARIATIONS ON A PHRASE BY CORMAC MCCARTHY"
Italicized passage: Cormac McCarthy, *The Crossing*, 1994.

"MELTING EQUESTRIAN"
"the sculptor": Meekyoung Shin, "Written in Soap" (2012). The original statue (of Prince William Augustus, Third Duke of Cumberland, on horseback, 1770) was removed in 1868.

"THE WAYFARER"
Exterior panels, *The Haywain Triptych* (1516). The earlier version of this image dates from circa 1500 and is rendered on a circular panel of oak.

"SLEEPING BEAR"
Section 2: Alan Kurdi, Omran Daqneesh.
Section 5: "Stroke of the pen": Executive Order 13769, January 27, 2017, summarily suspending the US Refugee Admissions Program and revoking the entry visas of travelers from seven Muslim-majority nations: Iran, Iraq, Libya, Somalia, Sudan, Syria, and Yemen. More than seven hundred travelers were detained, and up to sixty thousand visas "provisionally revoked."

"THE LONG RUN"

Section 1: First Platoon, Fourth Brigade Combat Team, 82nd Airborne Division, US Army. Veterans responding to the pardon of the man who ordered them to shoot innocent civilians in Afghanistan. Podcast, "The Cursed Platoon," *Washington Post*, July 2 and 3, 2020.

Section 2: "Fifteen steps": Carolyn McKinstry, speaking about her experience during the 1963 bombing of the Sixteenth Street Baptist Church in Birmingham, Alabama.

"NOT SO MUCH AN END AS AN ENTANGLING"

The title: Adapted from John Milton, *Tetrachordon*.

Italicized passages: *Paradise Lost*, Books VII and XI.

"HORSE IN A GAS MASK"

Babylon Berlin, season one (2017), title sequence and episode seven.

"FRAGMENT"

Wolfgang Amadeus Mozart, *Requiem in D Minor,* performed by the Oberlin College Orchestra and Choir, National Cathedral, Washington DC, May 10, 1970.

"his name": George Floyd.

"INTERIOR, 1917"

The photographs, drawn from the records of the National Woman's Party, can be found at http://hdl.loc.gov/loc.mss/mnwp.160045 and https://www.loc.gov/item/mnwp000237/.

"A KNITTED FEMUR"

Margaret Mead, responding to this question from a student: "What is the earliest sign of civilization?"

"SLIP"

Oscar Wilde, *Salomé*, directed by Owen Horsley, Stratford-upon-Avon, 2017. That year marked the fiftieth anniversary of the decriminalization of homosexuality in England and Wales.

"WHEN NOTHING BUT TREE"

A deep bow to Emma Mullaney and to Toby, for introducing me to the astonishing world of wilderness air scent search and rescue. And another to Peter Hughes, for so kindly inviting me to Switzerland in 1994 and showing me the wonders of the Kunstmuseum in Basel.

Acknowledgments

Grateful acknowledgment to the editors of the journals and anthologies in which the following poems first appeared, and to the organizations and individuals who kindly commissioned some of them.

- Academy of American Poets, *Poem-a-Day*: "Slip," "Interior, 1917," "Narrow Flame," "When Nothing but Tree"
- *The Atlantic*: "Variations on a Phrase by Corman McCarthy," "Deciduous"
- *Image*: "Scandinavian Grim," "Not So Much an End as an Entangling"
- *The Kenyon Review*: "Love Poem" (Emma), "Saint Sorry," "Environmental," "A Knitted Femur," "Uncorrected Vision," "Bearded Iris"
- *The London Review of Books*: "Archival," "Melting Equestrian"
- *The New Yorker*: "Love Poem" (Megan), "Horse in a Gas Mask"
- *Plume*: "The Wayfarer"
- *Poetry London* (UK): "Sleeping Bear"
- *Poetry Review* (UK): "Epithalamion"
- *The Yale Review*: "If the Cure for AIDS," "The Long Run"
- "Sleeping Bear" was jointly commissioned by the Academy of American Poets and the Library of Congress, to celebrate the hundredth anniversary of the establishment of the National Park Ser-

vice. Section 1 was translated into German by Ulrich Koch and published in *VERSschmuggel / reVERSible: Poetry from Germany and the USA,* ed. Karolina Golimowska, Alexander Gumz, and Thomas Wohlfahrt, Verlag das Wunderhorn, 2020. Section 2 was reprinted in *Staying Human*, ed. Neil Asley, Bloodaxe, 2020.

- "Deciduous" was commissioned by the Ohio Wesleyan chapter of Phi Beta Kappa. My thanks to David Caplan.
- "Not So Much an End as an Entangling" was commissioned by the Milton Society of America. My thanks to Elizabeth Sauer and Feisal Mohamed.
- "Interior, 1917" was jointly commissioned by the New York Philharmonic and the Academy of American Poets as part of Project 19, to mark the centennial of the Nineteenth Amendment to the US Constitution.
- "Ram of the Week" appeared in the e-book *Together in a Sudden Strangeness: American Poets Respond to the Pandemic*, ed. Alice Quinn, Knopf, 2020. "If the Cure for AIDS" appeared in the print version of this anthology.

Heartfelt thanks to:

Peggy McCracken and the University of Michigan's Institute for the Humanities for a fellowship that enabled me to complete this book.

Jericho Brown, Ilya Kaminsky, and everyone at the Haus für Poesie for inviting me to Berlin in 2019.

Jennifer Benka for presiding over the Academy of American Poets with such grace and passionate belief in poetry.

David Baker, Jericho Brown, Michael Collier, David Halperin, A. Van Jordan, Meghan O'Rourke, David St. John, Rosanna Warren, indispensable readers all.